The S

Contents

The Street	4
Doris Rules	12
The Whole Tooth	21
Vocabulary	30
Story Questions	32

Titles in the Runway series

Level 4	**Level 5**	**Level 6**
The Street	Trapped	The Good Student
The Wish	The Rumour	Virtual Teacher
The Magic Shop	The Food Museum	Football Smash
The Ghost House	Escape from the City	The Empty House

Badger Publishing Limited
Oldmedow Road, Hardwick Industrial Estate,
King's Lynn PE30 4JJ
Telephone: 01438 791037

www.badgerlearning.co.uk

8 10 9

The Street ISBN 978 1 84691 367 9

Text © Jane Langford, Melanie Joyce, Alison Hawes 2008
Complete work © Badger Publishing Limited 2008
Second edition © 2015

All rights reserved. No part of this publication may be reproduced, stored in any form or by any means mechanical, electronic, recording or otherwise without the prior permission of the publisher.

The right of Jane Langford, Melanie Joyce, and Alison Hawes to be identified as authors of this Work has been asserted by them in accordance with the Copyright, Designs and Patents Act 1988.

Publisher: David Jamieson
Commissioning Editor: Carrie Lewis
Design: Fiona Grant
Illustration: Paul Savage, Enzo Troiano, Robin Lawrie

The Street

Written by Jane Langford
Illustrated by Paul Savage

Abdi had no mum or dad.
He had no home.

But Abdi had his dog, Prince.
Abdi loved Prince and Prince loved Abdi.

One day Abdi saw his friend Hassan.
Hassan saw Abdi.

"Hi Abdi!" said Hassan.

But a car came.
It was going very fast!

The car was going to hit Hassan.

"Look out, Hassan!"
said Abdi.

Prince jumped at Hassan.
He saved Hassan, but the car hit Prince.

"I have no mum or dad. I have no home and now I have no Prince," said Abdi.

"Prince saved my life," said Hassan.
"You can come home with me."

The doorbell rang.
Mum opened the door.

Adou was nice to Aunty.
Mum was nice to Aunty.
But Aunty was never happy.

Adou went upstairs.
But Doris was not there.

Where is Doris?

Adou looked in the bedroom.
He looked in the bathroom.
He looked in the hall.

Aunty put her hat on.
She looked in the mirror…

Aunty ran away.

The Whole Tooth

Written by Alison Hawes
Illustrated by Robin Lawrie

Ryan and his brother Max went to the park.
Ryan wanted to play football.
His brother wanted to read his book.

Ryan shouted at Max.
"Come and play!"
"No," said Max.

Ryan was angry.
He didn't look where he was going.
He didn't see the goalpost.

Ryan's tooth fell out.

"Help!"

Max ran to Ryan.
"I know what to do," he said.

Max took the tooth to the park café.
He put the tooth in a cup of milk.

Then Max took Ryan to the dentist. The dentist put Ryan's tooth back in.

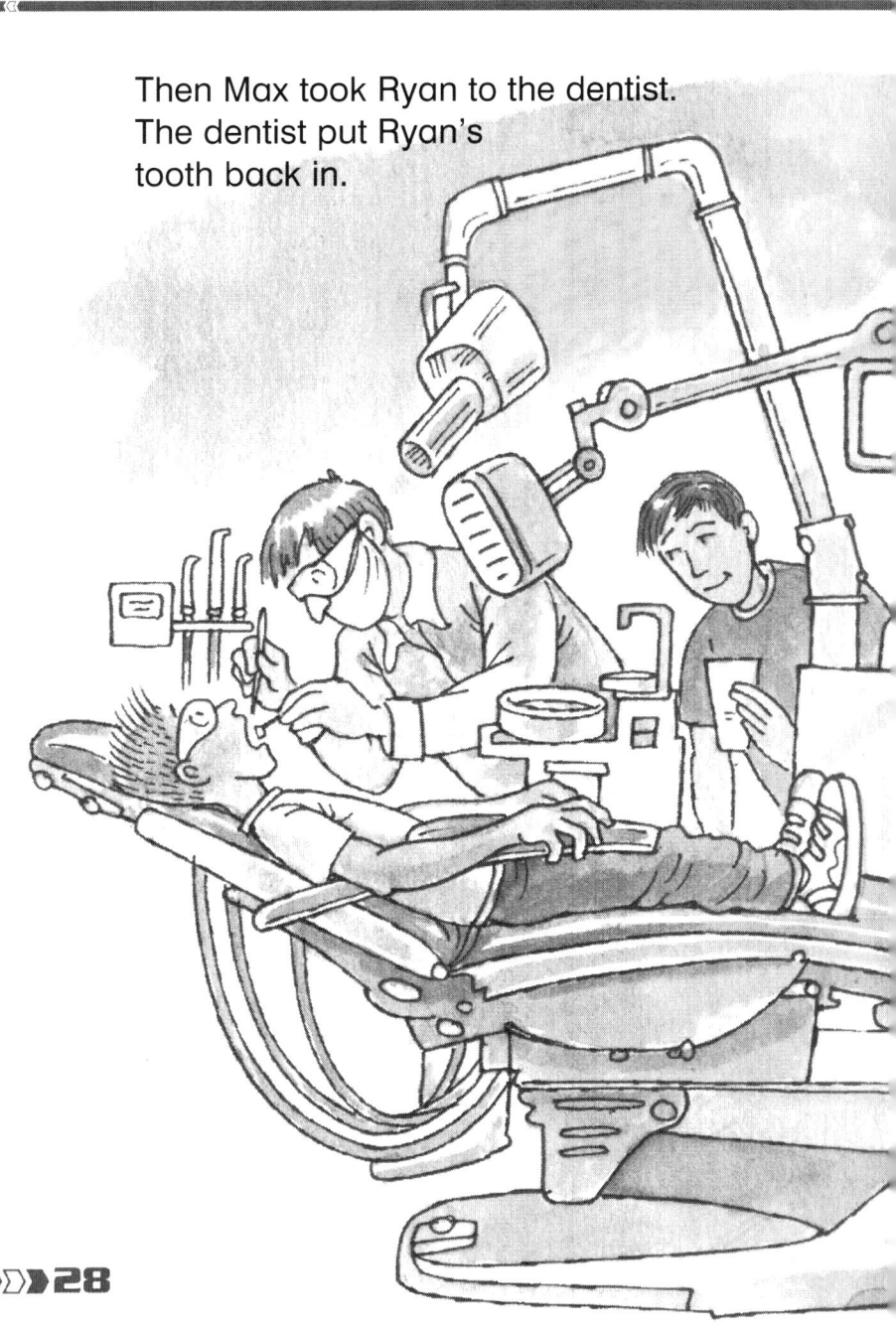

"How did you know what to do?" said Ryan.
"I read it in a book," laughed Max.

Vocabulary

The Street

mum
dad
home
loved
friend
Look out!
car
hit
jumped
saved

Doris Rules

aunty
mum
upstairs
doorbell
opened
bedroom
bathroom
hall
hat
mirror
forgot

The Whole Tooth

brother
angry
goalpost
tooth
cup
milk
dentist

>>> Story Questions

The Street

Does Abdi have a home?
Who saved Hassan?
What happened to Prince?

Doris Rules

Who was coming to stay?
Did Adou and his mum like Aunty?Did Aunty like Doris?

The Whole Tooth

What did Ryan want to do?
What happened to Ryan's tooth?
How did Max help?